WELCOME TO
THE WEDDING VISON

Mood Board

BOBANNA ART

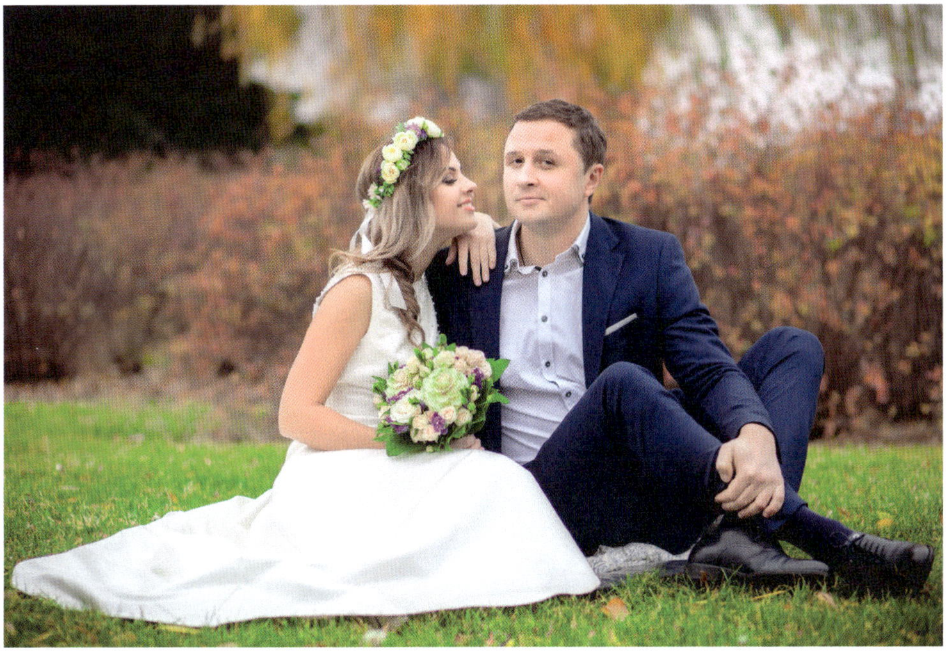

Thank you

Mr & Mrs. J Smith
Request the company of
at the marriage of their daughter
Sarah
to Mr. James Jones
on Saturday 15th August

Welcom
TO OUR WEDDI

M

Владислав
Мария
Wedding Ceremony

Printed in Great Britain
by Amazon

28628981R00027